Freshwater and Saltwater Habitats

Evie Golde

ROSEN
COMMON CORE
READERS

I0792481

Rosen Classroom™

New York

Published in 2014 by The Rosen Publishing Group, Inc.
29 East 21st Street, New York, NY 10010

Book Design: Mickey Harmon

Photo Credits: Cover, p. 7 Rich Carey/Shutterstock.com; p. 5 (pond) basel101658/Shutterstock.com; p. 5 (ocean) Pakhnyushcha/Shutterstock.com; p. 9 Anna Jurkovska/Shutterstock.com; p. 11 Darren J. Bradley/Shutterstock.com; p. 13 Pinosub/Shutterstock.com; p. 15 Tischenko Irina/Shutterstock.com; p. 17 Paul Whitted/Shutterstock.com; p. 19 cdelacy/Shutterstock.com; p. 21 Poznyakov/Shutterstock.com; p. 22 Clover/Shutterstock.com.

ISBN: 978-1-4777-2379-1
6-pack ISBN: 978-1-4777-2380-7

Manufactured in the United States of America

CPSIA Compliance Information: Batch #CS13RC: For further information contact Rosen Publishing, New York, New York at 1-800-237-9932.

Contents

Earth's Water

What do you see when you look at a map of Earth? You might notice that there's much more water than land. That's because most of Earth is covered with water! It includes everything from ponds to oceans.

There are two kinds of water on Earth: freshwater and salt water. Although they're different, they're both habitats. Many different creatures call freshwater and salt water home.

A habitat is a place where a plant or animal lives in nature.

freshwater

salt water

Ecosystems

Freshwater and salt water both contain ecosystems. An ecosystem is a community of living and nonliving things. All living things in the ecosystem depend on each other to live.

Every part of an ecosystem affects everything else around it. Freshwater and salt water are different, so plants and animals in those ecosystems are different, too.

An ocean is only one example of an ecosystem.

All About Freshwater

Freshwater comes from Earth's rainwater and melted ice. It makes up only a tiny bit of Earth's water. People need freshwater for drinking, but it's also home to many cool creatures!

One type of freshwater habitat is a pond. A pond is a body of water that's surrounded by land. Some ponds are big, and others are small. You may even have one in your backyard!

Ponds are usually still on the surface, but there's a whole world underneath to learn about!

Lily pads grow in ponds. They can live only in freshwater. That's because the system that carries water throughout the plant can't **process** a lot of salt.

Lily pads give small animals food and a place to hide. They have special **adaptations** to help them live in freshwater habitats. For example, their long, thin stems put the leaves above water so they can get sun.

A lily pad's roots hold it in the bottom of the pond, while its leaves sit on top of the water to take in sun.

leaves
stem

The plants in a habitat affect the kinds of animals that live there. That's because certain animals only eat certain plants. So animals must live in habitats where there's food.

Some fish can only live in freshwater. Like lily pads, their bodies can't process salt. Freshwater fish breathe by passing water through their **gills**. Having salt water pass through their gills would hurt them.

Trout and catfish are two kinds of freshwater fish.

brown trout

All About Salt Water

Most of Earth's water is salt water. It's found in our oceans and seas. The salt in the water comes from many places. Rivers and wind carry salt to the oceans and seas.

Another way salt water is made is when salt from deep inside Earth comes up through openings in the bottom of oceans and seas.

Water bugs, many kinds of fish, dolphins, and whales are all part of ocean ecosystems.

Kelp is a kind of algae (AL-jee) found in many oceans. Its stems can be hundreds of feet long. Its leaves have tiny air pouches under them that hold them up toward the sun. These things help kelp stay alive underwater.

Many animals use kelp as food and as a place to hide from bigger animals. In this way, it helps the animals in an ocean ecosystem stay alive.

All the kelp in one area is called a kelp forest.

Like freshwater fish, saltwater fish breathe with gills. However, their bodies can process the salt in the water. Some saltwater fish are small, such as clown fish. Others, like great white sharks, are huge!

Fish eat plants and other fish in the ecosystem. This keeps oceans from becoming overcrowded. If there were too many animals in the ocean, the food would run out.

Fish aren't the only animals in a saltwater habitat. Whales, sea lions, seals, and sea turtles live there, too.

Keep It Clean

Freshwater and saltwater habitats are very different, but they're both important. They give our world many interesting plants and animals. They're a great way to learn about the **connections** between living things.

We can take care of Earth's water by keeping it clean and respecting the living creatures that call it home. All Earth's water is important to having a healthy planet!

Water is just as important to people as it is to plants and animals.

Who Lives Underwater?

Freshwater	Salt Water
trout	dolphins
catfish	sharks
bugs	coral
pond algae	clown fish
lily pads	sea turtles
pond turtles	kelp
frogs	turtle grass

Glossary

adaptation (aa-dap-TAY-shun) A change that helps a living creature live better in its environment.

connection (kuh-NEK-shun) A link between two creatures in an ecosystem.

gill (GIHL) The body part a fish uses to breathe underwater.

process (PRAH-sehs) To deal with.

Index